My Name is Zuma

A Story about Autism

Written by: **Isaac Osae-Brown**   Illustrated by: **George Franco**

To order additional copies of this book, contact:
Xlibris
1-888-795-4274
www.Xlibris.com
Orders@Xlibris.com

ISBN: Softcover   978-1-7960-5269-5
         Hardcover   978-1-7960-5270-1
         EBook   978-1-7960-5268-8

Library of Congress Control Number: 2019911806

Print information available on the last page

Rev. date: 10/29/2019

To my wife Obioma, my beloved Jordan and Nanaba who inspire me to keep loving.

To my teacher and mentor, Caron Mellblom-Nishioka Ed.D whose contribution brought this book to life.

To all who remain heroes for Autism.

FOR ALL PARENTS AND EDUCATORS

Autism, also called Autism Spectrum Disorder (ASD) is a developmental disorder that may impair the ability to communicate and interact. It typically appears during the first three years of life. Autism is not a mental illness and individuals with autism should not be misconstrued as such. At first glance, a person with autism may appear to have a mental, learning, and hearing disability. It is important therefore to distinguish autism from other conditions and seek for an accurate diagnosis to provide the basis for building appropriate and effective treatment programs. Research reveals that treatment can assist individuals with learning to manage their behaviors, but this condition cannot be cured.

Many who read this book may come in contact with individuals with autism like Zuma. It will be helpful to equip yourselves with adequate information about autism and know how to communicate effectively and build relationship to encourage socialization.

STORY SUMMARY

Zuma is a 12-year-old boy with autism, from California. Sometimes, Zuma feels discouraged because he is not as popular among the kids in his community. His potential is trapped; locked inside his mind. While other kids can describe their thoughts with words, Zuma thinks in pictures. He struggles with words, and has a hard time expressing himself. His dad is stressed out, and unhappy. Luckily, help comes from professionals who know the perfect strategy to bring out Zuma's potential to read, speak, and play. They understand that Zuma is not the only one who is different; everyone is. They help Zuma and his family to understand that individuals with disabilities are just as capable as everyone else. Zuma confronts his fears, and ultimately, sets the stage for inclusive education.

My name is Zuma. I do not behave like other kids.

When I was three, I didn't have a whole lot of words to say.

I get mad. I hit other kids and scream a lot. I always get in trouble.

I make messes and I can't help it.

I don't like people to touch me because that makes me nervous.

I only like to wear one outfit because other things look funny on my body. I don't know how to tell anybody about how I feel.

Everybody thinks I look weird because I flap my hands a lot.

When other kids are playing together in group games, I only stay in the corner and play alone with my toy train. I can't stay calm; I wish I could.

Ada, my big sister can cook and Tami, my little sister likes to skip and to read.

Why can't I do all these things?

My parents were worried about me so they took me to the doctor.

Silly tests were taken and many questions were asked.

I didn't want to talk to the doctor.

At the end, he told my parents that I had Autism. My dad asked what that meant.

"Well, your boy is not talking and doesn't know how to play with other kids his age and make friends. This is all what autism is about." The doctor said.

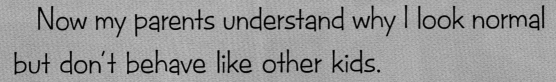

Now my parents understand why I look normal but don't behave like other kids.

I don't understand what is wrong with me.

My first day at school was really scary! I was alone and didn't want to play with anyone.

I stayed in the corner the whole day!

Other kids stared at me. I wanted to make friends but I had no idea, how to do that.

They don't see me do normal things. I can't ride a bike, jump, climb or dance. When I try, I fall over.

I don't like to look at people in the eye. When I do, I see lots of people. This is confusing!

I can't read like the other kids. Letters jump
when I read and numbers looked backwards!

The kids in my class are really good at reading.

They laugh and stare when I'm called on to read.

I am sad and don't know what to do. When the kids laugh at me, I get mad.

People even think that I'm no good.

I can't change who I am, but ordinary people can!

My parents help me to follow directions and to respect other kids.

I can do what other kids do if everyone can learn to accept the way I am.

Now, I have a new school with other kids who behave like me.

I have many toys to play with. I even have an iPad to play bingo games.

Parties and fieldtrips with other kids are scary but my teachers help me to keep calm.

There is one girl who doesn't seem to mind how I act. She will come over with another toy and play with me sometimes. I like that, but I'm not sure what to do.

It's cool when people play with others who are not like them.

My teachers make me read and write letters on a straight line. The letters I see, seem to look right. Now, I get it! I can read and write with the other kids.

I'm no longer a mess. I draw trains and make kites for fun! The other kids like my kites.

If everyone can love me and play with me, I will do well and not be afraid. I have autism and I cannot change who I am.

Sometimes I feel ok, but other days are a mess.

I need help!

If you all help me to do right, you'll see the beauty in my mind.

I'm one of the world's natural wonders.

RESOURCES FOR PARENTS

Autism Speaks.

https://www.autismspeaks.org

Autism Society of America.

http://www.autism-society.org

Council for Exceptional Children.

https://www.cec.sped.org/

Printed in the United States
By Bookmasters